TANTRIC SEX

Step-by-Step Guide to Learning the Art of Tantric Sex!

Grace Mason & Jim Owens

Table of Contents

Introduction

I would like to thank you for purchasing this book.

Sex is a vital part of life, and it is an activity that needs to be performed by adults not just for their physical well-being, but for their mental well-being as well. In today's world, where we have all grown accustomed to our incredibly hectic lifestyles, even 24 hours don't seem sufficient. Trying to juggle between their work and social life, more often than not, people tend to give up on their sex lives. Sexless marriages have been growing at an alarming rate in the recent past, where the couple engages in little or even no sex. Sex is essential for having a psychologically and physically nourishing relationship.

One way in which the sexual spark can be reignited in a relationship is by making use of a technique that is referred to as "Tantra." Practicing Tantra will help a couple in communicating better and also assist them in attaining greater pleasure. Tantric sex is a sexual activity wherein the couples engage in various sexually and emotionally satisfying experiences that will help in the amalgamation of their souls.

This book will help you and your partner with getting started on an adventurous journey towards attaining the ultimate sexual pleasure imaginable. You will be able to revolutionize your sex life with the secrets of Tantra, and it will help you in attaining sexual, spiritual and emotional fulfillment. It will help in connecting with your partner, tapping into the innate energy present within your body and revel in orgasms like never before. You and your partner will be able to discover the different ways in which you will be able to experience physical pleasure by doing the simplest things, like synchronized breathing, gentle caressing and just holding each other.

You might want to try your hand at Tantric sex for bringing back some excitement to your love life, or you may be simply curious about Tantra. Tantric sex will change your perspective towards sex, regardless of your reason for trying it out. This book will provide you with all the information that you will need about Tantra and the various aspects of tantric sex. The topics covered in this book include the history and meaning of Tantra, the different benefits of tantric sex, different tantric sex positions, Tantric exercises and so on. It provides a wholesome and holistic experience for the couple. If you want to see some positive results, then you will need to put in considerable time and effort.

Without any further ado, let's get started! All the best!

Chapter 1: What Is Tantra And Tantric Sex?

Before getting started with tantric sex, it is crucial to understand the concept of Tantra. The practice of Tantra can be traced back to ancient India, where several saints and holy men used to engage in various ritualistic and meditational techniques. This technique is believed to have been in existence since the 5th century A.D., and it was perceived as a method that would help an individual harness divine consciousness as well as their conscience. This concept traveled across the globe and resulted in the modern day usage of the term Tantra assuming a new meaning altogether. The term Tantra is popularly associated with the practice of Tantric sex. This involves engaging in a sexual act with the intent of garnering divine consciousness together. To put it simply, tantric sex is a practice that is made use of for reaching sexual nirvana.

History of Tantra

There is some obscurity regarding the origin of the concept

of tantric sex, but it is a popular belief that a community, referred to as the "Lemurian" people were considered to be the first people to practice this particular form of sacred sex. They considered the human body as a divine vessel and made use of various stimulating techniques for engaging the senses in order to reel in spiritual liberation. Some people tend to believe that Tantra is related to the ancient Indian practice of "yoga" as well, since these two techniques make use of different bodily postures for forming a bond with the Cosmos.

Tantric sex has gained a lot of popularity in the recent past and it has become popular in the western world with a lot of celebrities like Sting, Madonna and even the late Steve Jobs who had admitted to having tried this technique. Now, it has slowly found acceptance all over the world. Several purists do believe in its effectiveness in achieving greater pleasure.

Tantric sex satisfies people physically, mentally and spiritually as well. Tantric sex provides complete satisfaction and makes the entire body feel extremely pleasurable, helps in emotionally connecting with one's partner and on a spiritual level; it helps in the amalgamation of two souls and brings them closer to divinity.

Tantra makes use of two energies; the female and the male energies. The female energy is referred to as Shakti, and the male energy is known as Shiva. Shakti and Shiva are Hindu gods, and their idol worship involves the worshipping of Ling and Yon. Linga means the penis and yon means the vagina. When a couple engages in tantric sex, then the female energy present in the body, Shakti, rises through the different chakras, and it pierces through the female center that's referred to as the Kundalini and then it merges with the male energy, referred to as Shiva. This fusion of energies helps in forming a bond that surpasses the mortal realm.

Various aspects of Tantric Sex

There are three main important aspects of Tantric sex, and these are tantric communication, tantric positions and tantric exercising. Tantric communication is a process that helps in the merging of a couple emotionally and mentally. This helps in bringing them close to one another and is capable of turning a regular couple into soul mates. Tantric positions are certain positions that will help in bringing a couple together sexually. There are different tantric exercises as well as breathing techniques that will help in reaping the most out of tantric sex. More information about these three aspects of Tantric sex has been explained in the coming chapters.

Tantric sex does help in freeing the body, mind and soul. This is possible through the practice of the techniques as mentioned above. Calming one's mind is a crucial aspect of any practice that involves meditation. Similarly, for practicing tantric sex, it is critical to ease your mind. These techniques have been mentioned in the book.

Unlike regular sex, the teachings of tantric sex concentrate on making the participants aware of their actions while involved in a sexual act with their partner. If you are mindful of your actions, then you can ensure that you can induce a feeling of reverence and even respect for your partner. It is about honoring your body and that of your partner's as well. The primary objective of tantric sex is to help you relax your body and mind. When you can find this release, you will be able to express yourself with an unbridled ease that will deepen and strengthen the bond that exists between you and your partner; the kind of love that would unify your souls.

Tantric sex helps you heal

Perhaps one of the greatest possible uses of tantric sex is that it can help in healing your body and soul. It will also help you to let go of unwanted thoughts and make your mind feel lighter. You might have been hurt in the past or might have endured some form of rejection in your previous relationships. Tantric sex will help you in forgiving yourself and will help you to learn to love yourself once again and to cherish your body as you were meant to. Different techniques have been mentioned in this book that will help you in healing and freeing yourself from any guilt or trauma that you might have endured. You will notice that you will be feeling more empowered if you follow the advice that's been given in this book. Tantric sex will indeed help you heal and it is done through the following steps. You will need to identify the incident that has hurt you in the past. This hurt could have been real or imaginary. Therefore, the next step would be to determine whether it was real or imaginary. Sexual stimulation will help you in identifying the difference. You will be able to find the negative emotions attached to this particular hurt and can let them go. Replace these negative feelings with positive emotions and experiences that will help you heal.

Tantric sex is indeed magical. You will find that the various techniques that have been mentioned in this book will not only help you in letting go of your fears and hurt, but they will also help you in expressing yourself better. Also, as an added benefit these techniques will help you in feeling younger and more relaxed.

Myths and Truths about Tantric Sex and Tantra

Tantra is about celebrating sexuality and sensuality. It is a general misconception that Tantra is all about sex. Without being fully aware of the Tantra, people have been known to criticize it. This section helps in uncovering all the myths that are associated with Tantric sex and Tantra.

Myth #1: Tantric sex is only about sex.

Truth: Tantric sex does involve sexual intercourse, but it isn't all about genital contact. Tantric sex is all about the union of the souls and not just the bodies. Genital contact or sex will only help in increasing this connection between the souls. However, this is done only when the couple is comfortable with each other and is ready for that level of intimacy. Tantric sex involves various aspects that have absolutely nothing to do with sex.

Myth #2: If you start practicing Tantra, then you are simply giving up on pleasure.

Truth: This myth is loosely based on the previous myth. It is simply a myth. The teaching of Tantra don't include the renouncing of sexual pleasure, like some of the yogic practices do. Tantra simply enhances the level of pleasure that you can experience. Tantric sex theory does not mention that you need to deny your desires. In fact, Tantric sex encourages the free expression of your sexual desires. You don't have to mimic a yogi, sit cross-legged or meditate for ages for forming a connection with the Cosmos. Tantra realizes the importance of sex in an individual's life and it helps in the harnessing of the dormant sexual energy present in the body for attaining bliss. This bliss that can be attained is beyond anything present in the physical realm.

Myth #3: Tantric sex increases your sexual appetite and the need for seeking pleasure that leads to affairs.

Truth: Tantric sex does not increase your sexual appetite or lead you astray in your search for pleasure. Instead, it will help you in controlling your desires and will also help in channeling the sexual energy that is present within your body for a higher purpose. You might have not even been aware of your true potential. Tantric sex does not encourage engaging in sex with multiple partners. This assumption has somehow made its way into the minds of many and is wrong. As mentioned earlier, Tantric sex will help you in forming a strong physical and emotional bond with your partner and simply deepen the spiritual commitment that exists between you. Sexuality isn't something that should be thrown around mindlessly; it needs to be honored and cherished for attaining a higher level of consciousness. It is not about rushing towards an orgasm, but it is about learning to control yourself and your desires. This will help in forming a stronger attachment towards your partner. You will be able to form a relationship that isn't based on physical needs.

Myth #4: It will turn you into a nymphomaniac.

Truth: Well, this isn't true, and it is quite silly. Tantric sex does help in releasing all the sexual energy present in the body and it also does enable you to express yourself as freely as possible, but this doesn't mean that it will turn you into a nymphomaniac. However, there are chances that this can be misused. With practice, you will be able to control your desires and stop enjoying meaningless sex.

These common myths have marred the image of Tantric sex in the minds of the general public. It isn't a taboo and should be practiced freely if that is your choice.

The Ten pledges of Tantra

Once you have made up your mind to follow the teachings of Tantric sex, then there are ten pledges that you will need to remember. Before getting started, it is important that you know what these pledges are. You should feel a sense of peace while saying these pledges. The ten pledges are as follows:

1. I pledge to discover the divinity that exists within my body.

2. I pledge to respect and pursue the Gods and Goddesses that exist within my body and that of my partner's as well.

3. I pledge to explore not just my sexuality but my sensuality as well, for making sure that none of my chakras are being blocked because of any emotions.

4. I pledge to strike a balance between my soul, relationships and my surroundings.

5. I pledge to make use of this balance for ensuring that the rest of the world is at peace as well.

6. I pledge to not only understand but also explore my sensuality for ensuring that there's harmony in my relationships.

7. I pledge to make sure that all the emotional baggage and blockages that exist due to my past or even my present have been removed. I will free my spirit and express myself without any restrictions.

8. I pledge to work towards reconnecting with my inner child.

9. I pledge to love and heal my partner and myself as well.

10. I pledge to make use of the rejuvenated sexual energy for making myself more confident, gentle and connect with my partner and those around me.

You have to participate and observe

As mentioned earlier, you will need to make sure that your mind is calm and quiet for practicing tantric sex. This is the only way in which you will be able to be a participant and an observer as well. This means that you will need to be observing not just your actions but those of your partner as well while you are engaged in lovemaking.

Once you start paying attention to your actions, then you are a witness. This will help you in letting go of any anxiety that you might be experiencing. When an individual is making love, regardless of their sex, there would be a million thoughts and doubts going through their minds. They would worry about whether or not they can please their partner. Does their partner like what they are doing? Are they are doing it right? These questions add to the anxiety levels and take away from the potential of relaxation. Once you start following the teaching of Tantric sex, then you will be able to witness yourself while engaged in this act. Here are some techniques that will help you in being both a participant as well as an observer.

Mantras

Have you ever been so bored that you simply start humming a particular sound continuously? Did this seem to have some hypnotic effect on you? Mantras are quite similar to this. They are silent or even spoken sounds and they elicit a particular reaction from the body because of their vibrations. These vibrations correspond with all the seven chakras that are present in the body. If you have never experienced this before, then try saying "Om" and draw in deep breaths that would correspond with this "Om." You will notice that you can calm yourself down and are also able to focus your mind. You will be able to control the movement of energy that's present within your body. A mantra has the same effect on your mind and your way of thinking as your favorite music does. You will be able to calm yourself down. When you make use of mantras, your mind can wander wherever it pleases and take you along.

The sounds that you make while saying a mantra are short and repetitive in nature. This repetition makes them have a hypnotic effect. A mantra can be a single word, a sentence or even a verse. If you don't know any mantras, then you can make one up on your own. It could even be a sound that you like.

Yantras

A yantra is a mathematical technique that's often used in Tantric sex. You might not be fond of mathematics, but you should be aware that geometric figures are critical when it comes to Tantric sex. You will need to focus on the image if you want to stimulate your sexuality and a precise figure needs to be kept in mind for eliciting a particular reaction. If you are feeling nervous or even anxious while engaging in sexual intercourse, you can focus on such figures for letting go of all the negative emotions. Different geometric figures are related to each of the seven chakras that are present within the human body. These chakras are the vortices for energy that's stored in the body. One of the famous Yantras is the sex point Star of David.

Things that you should know about Tantric sex

Everyone will have heard about Tantric sex at one point in time or another, and from various sources. There's a lot of information available about Tantric sex, and this leads to a lot of confusion. Therefore, it is quite natural that you are confused about what Tantric sex is all about. The reason for this is quite simple; the way it has been portrayed on TV and movies is quite different from what it's actually like. Therefore, it is no surprise that most people are misinformed about what Tantric sex comprises. Not just this, but there's a stigma that is associated with Tantric sex. It is considered to be a weird form of pornography or even voodoo! All this isn't true and is baseless. Tantric sex is based on the teachings of Tantra. Tantra is an ancient art form that is based on the principles of attaining fulfillment and enlightenment, about living life to the fullest and living it without any unnecessary societal constraints. Tantric sex isn't a crazy practice, and it will, in fact, help you form a more meaningful and stronger bond with your partner. A couple will be able to experience sexual intimacy like never before. In this section, you will learn what Tantric sex is all about.

It's more than just sex

As mentioned earlier, Tantric sex isn't simply about sex. This does come as a surprise to many. The physical aspect of sex includes touching, rubbing and petting. You will have engaged in all this while having regular sex. Then what's the difference between Tantric sex and regular sex? Tantric sex gives equal importance to not just the physical aspect of sex, but also the importance of partners being connected on a mental level too. It would be quite helpful if you and your partner could forget about achieving an orgasm, and could instead shift your focus towards the act that you are involved. When you let go of all expectations, you will be able to direct all your energy towards enjoying the moment and appreciating each other as well. It will help in creating an intimacy that surpasses all the physical bonds and connects with each other spiritually. This makes Tantric sex so much better than its regular counterpart does.

It can help in healing you

Regular sex has the capacity for satisfying your physical needs and urges, but Tantric sex can help in satisfying your emotional needs as well. All the traumatic experiences that you might have endured in the past, your fears and insecurities that you have can be done away with the use of Tantric sex. Tantric sex makes use of different meditational techniques, focuses on your breathing and also maintaining eye contact with your partner and doing other little things that will make sex so much better than it ever was. This will also help in achieving a healthier and happier state of being. The gentle touches of Tantric sex will help in forming a stronger bond with your partner and wash away all your unpleasant emotions and experiences.

Achieving full body orgasms

A full-body orgasm might seem quite interesting and dubious at the same time. Well, Tantric sex will help you achieve this. The pleasure that you can experience while engaging in Tantric sex is higher than regular sex. The reason for this is that, when practiced properly, it can indeed help in achieving a full body orgasm, and this is quite natural. This happens when you start focusing on spreading the dormant sexual energy that is present in your body to all the cells in the body instead of simply restricting it to your genitals. This will intensify the pleasure you are experiencing and make your body come alive.

It can be challenging

Tantric sex is not always easy to perform. Regardless of whether or not you have known your partner all your life, it can still be quite challenging. You will need a little more focus and practice in order to get the hang of tantric sex. Tantric sex is a pristine form of lovemaking, and in order to enjoy all its benefits, it is important that the people who are engaging in it are able to let go of all their inhibitions fully. There isn't a quick or an easy way in which you will be able to get the hang of it. You will need to let go of all the previous notions of lovemaking that you might have had and redefine this entire process. You can start out by sitting on the bed or any comfortable surface and gaze into each other's eyes. It is about forming a bond with your partner and maintaining a connection with your partner throughout the duration of sexual intercourse.

There are Tantric sex courses available as well. Before you get any wrong ideas, these courses aren't group orgies, nor do they include any graphic demonstrations. These are classes that will teach a couple to connect with each other on a deeper level and help in forming a bond that transcends the physical world. Various topics are covered in these courses, and these can be practiced with your partner within the sanctity and privacy of your own home. There are online courses available as well. Once you have got the hang of the basics, you can engage in some mind-blowing sex.

Chapter 2: Benefits of Tantric Sex

As already mentioned in the previous chapter, Tantric sex will help in bringing two people closer together and help in their spiritual, emotional and mental union. In this chapter, you will learn about the various benefits that Tantric sex has on offer.

Individual growth

Tantric sex helps in increasing the intimacy quotient in a relationship. It also helps in the growth of individuals as well. A person would be able to grow mentally, physically, as well as spiritually. Tantric sex helps in awakening Kundalini in women, and this allows for her feminine nature to shine through. She will start to glow and have a more positive outlook and attitude towards life. The male energy, Shiva helps a man to harness all his masculine energy through peace and inner strength.

Exploring the limits

Quickies and self-pleasuring techniques are becoming quite common these days, and people are more often than not missing out on the benefits that meaningful and loving sex can provide. This hinders an individual from exploring their sexual limits. Tantric sex can help turn this around. Tantric sex would help an individual in understanding their true sexuality and their sexual limits. When a couple engages in Tantric sex, they form a deep and meaningful bond that allows each partner to experience sexual bliss. Tantric sex can be thought of like a team effort where each partner helps the other reach and reel in great physical, emotional and sexual pleasure that can be experienced by both.

Heightened orgasms

The orgasms achieved through Tantric sex are more powerful than the ordinary ones. The various tantric sex positions mentioned in this book will help you in achieving earth-shattering orgasms. The positions are designed such that they hit all the sweet spots and make your body sing. It is a general notion that women can have a higher level of orgasm when compared to men, but with Tantric sex, both men and women can achieve a higher state of orgasm.

Knowing what works

Once you have managed to get the hang of it, Tantric sex can be enjoyable and exciting. With each successive session, you will get a better understanding of your sexuality, your triggers and also those of your partner. You will be able to understand what you and your partner enjoy. Once you have managed to identify these pleasure points, you can start stimulating them for achieving pure sexual bliss. The physical and mental bond that you would have established with your partner would simply depend on him and strengthen over a period and you will reach a stage where you, as a couple, become dependent on each other's sexual energy for their pleasure.

Timed bliss

You can time your orgasms with Tantric sex. Once an individual has managed to gain control over their mind as well as body, they can automatically fall into a synchronized pattern for attaining a mutual orgasm. A new form of energy is generated, and it flows through each of them when they have timed orgasms. This does amplify the bond between couples. Teachings of Tantric sex suggest that staying connected after a sexual act will help in strengthening the bond that's formed.

Monogamy

It is a popular belief that Tantric sex can help a couple in staying together for the rest of their lifespan. When two individuals have managed to forge a bond that helps them to connect on a deeper plane, they become dependent. This dependency cannot be mimicked or replicated with anyone else. When the frequency of the session starts to increase, then the bond between the individuals also starts to deepen and strengthen.

Health benefits

Tantric sex does help in promoting good health. Women will benefit from this because it will help in making their menstrual cycle more regular and this, in turn, helps them in keeping their bodies in good shape. Tantric sex helps in producing certain male hormones that produce healthier and stronger sperms, thereby increasing the couple's fertility. A full body orgasm helps in fueling the body cells and also helps in increasing their strength to combat disease, thereby increasing the immunity. Women and men who have Tantric sex tend to look younger because this is a great stress buster.

It also adds a new glow to the face. Apart from all the various benefits that it has to offer everyone, Tantric sex can also help in producing serotonin that assists in keeping depression at bay. An orgasm helps in releasing serotonin that helps in keeping cortisol at bay and improves an individual's mood.

Inhibitions

It also helps in making a person get accustomed to their body and be more comfortable with their body and that of their partner. Most people in this day and age tend to get extremely conscious about their bodies and these fears that they harbor stop them from thoroughly enjoying sex and they end up having mediocre sex. Once you let go of the fear of being judged and have accepted your body for the way it is, then you will be able to truly let go and savor the moment, as it was meant to be enjoyed. If you let go of all these fears, you can enjoy physical pleasure. Letting go of your inhibitions will make sex more enjoyable. Tantric sex encourages this abandonment.

Power struggle

If you follow the popular television series "The Game of Thrones," then you will remember the episode where Daenerys Targaryen breaks all the norms and decides to take charge of pleasuring her alpha-male husband, Khal Drogo. Drogo objects at first, but then he gives in once he realizes how pleasurable it really is. When it comes to sex, more often than not, people tend to face an inner power struggle. Men and women both tend to like the feeling of being in control, through showing that they are in control can do serious damage to a relationship. There is a difference between being in control and enjoying mutual Tantric sex. Tantric sex will help in eliminating this problem altogether. Tantric sex gives equal power to both the partners and the different positions will help in allowing both the parties to be in charge and they can give each pleasure the other person without any restrictions.

Happiness

Tantric sex helps in channeling all the positive forms of energy and this will help in making the individual extremely happy. Since it is spiritually, emotionally and physically satisfying, an individual would be happy in all these aspects. The spiritual connection that it lets you form with divinity helps.

Increased love

There are thousands of thoughts that go through your mind at any given point of time. We tend to think about different people, not necessarily our partners. It's quite common these days for couples to break off their relationships on the pretext that they aren't feeling "the love" anymore. Tantric sex will not only help you in loving yourself, but it will also help you in loving your partner. It helps in developing a nurturing relationship that helps in mutual growth. This kind of strength of feeling makes the relationship more solid.

Empowers both men and women

Most women tend to suffer from low self-esteem. They have become plagued with thoughts and feelings that their bodies are imperfect. They may not have the power to say no to their partner while engaged in a sexual act. They may not be truly willing to have sex but are forced into it because of their inability to say no. They might not express their true feelings and desires freely, and this reduces the pleasure that they experience. According to the teachings of Tantric sex, women are treated like goddesses, and they are showered with the attention and the respect that they deserve. Likewise, even men are plagued with different issues regarding the way they perceive themselves. Most men worry about the way they are performing, whether or not they can satisfy their partner if their stamina is good enough and so on and so forth. Instead of enjoying the act, they are often worried about how long they can last. When they follow the teachings of Tantric sex, they will feel empowered since their bodies are honored as the vessels of God. This will make them more confident and open to new experiences without having to live with those fears and inhibitions.

Immense satisfaction

There are times when you might have had sex and felt that something was missing in it. You might feel that there's no excitement or romance. This tends to happen since sex doesn't go beyond intercourse. It stops at the physical act. Sex alone does not do anything for a relationship. Tantric sex is more pleasurable since it helps in forming an emotional bond between partners instead of a simple physical bond. When a person is emotionally invested in an act, it becomes more pleasurable and enjoyable. When both are, it becomes magical.

Alleviates depression

Think of Tantric sex as your counselor. It will help you in overcoming depression and even anxiety. People are usually too tired to eat or sleep these days. This wreaks havoc on their daily schedule. Tantric sex will help you in tackling the problems mentioned above. After a session of Tantric sex, you will feel revitalized and reenergized, and this newfound peace and energy will relax your body and calm your mind, thereby getting rid of all the unnecessary tensions that keep stressing you.

Tantric sex is so much more than just sex!

Chapter 3: The Basics of Tantric Sex

When you start to follow the teachings of Tantric sex, then you will start to notice a positive change in yourself. You will notice a change in the way you view yourself and also see a positive shift in your outlook towards life in general. You will find yourself looking at long-term relationships instead of instant gratification.

You will learn that every individual has a certain level of divinity that is present within him or her and that this is a given. This change in your perspective will make you view sex as a sacred act and not just a physical one. You will also learn to find and forge a deeper connection with your partner and attain a greater level of pleasure. You will be successful only when you have relieved yourself of any preconceived notions that you might have. You should stop thinking about what you should do to please your lover or what your lover has got to do to pleasure you. After reading this chapter, you will be able to identify certain different ideas that you might have about yourself and also learn how to let go to have great sex. This chapter will help you in understanding the basic concepts of Tantric sex.

The Yin and the Yang

You must have heard the phrase that men are from Mars and women are from Venus. It is perceived that men are more assertive and powerful, while women tend to be more soft, fragile and nurturing in nature. Several other stereotypes exist; men are not capable of expressing their feeling while women tend to have a plethora of emotions that are simply waiting to be unleashed at any second. Another general misconception is that women don't normally like to take credit for the work they do because this is a trait associated with men since they are more outgoing. Over the last few years, there's been a drastic change in the way both men and women think.

The principles of Tantric sex firmly believe that men and women are different and that they have opposing characteristics. This is a very basic principle of Tantra and is embodied in the Eastern principal Yin and Yang. Yin represents feminism, and Yang represents masculinity. However, this doesn't mean that women aren't capable of possessing and Yang characteristics and likewise. Rather than thinking of men and women as two entities, focusing on their energies is a good idea. Tantra firmly believes in the merging of the energies of these two entities.

Shiva and Shakti

One of the most common images of Yin and Yang can be found in Hindu mythical literature. Yin and Yang are represented by the divine couple of Lord Shiva and Goddess Shakti. Lord Shiva is considered to be the energy that is present in the universe and Shakti is seen as the source of all this energy. The union of these two powerful deities is responsible for creating the longing in you and everybody else for being to be treated like a God or Goddess. This has been discussed in the coming chapters. You will discover how to worship your partner as a God or a Goddess.

The masculine energy that is found in Lord Shiva is ecstasy, whereas the feminine energy that is present in Goddess Shakti represents wisdom. The balanced combination of these two results in enlightenment. This couple is always represented in various positions where they are entwined in one form or another. They are dancing, embracing, or standing together closely. There are also some positions where Shakti is wrapped around Shiva, and her legs are propped up around his hips. Their dancing position is by far considered to be the most sacred one since they are not only able to free their energies but are also able to attain enlightenment.

Understanding the opposites

There might be some divisions that exist between you and your partner. The first thing that you will have to do is identify these divisions and then strike a balance between the two opposing forces of energy that exist within. There might be a few stereotypical characteristics that you might have noticed. Take a note of these and also ask your partner to do this as well. You will then have to figure out the way in which you can embrace these traits about yourself and also learn to love your partner fully. Only when you can strike a balance between these polarities that exist between you two, only then will you be able to find a perfect balance. You will have to identify the Yin to your partner's Yang and he has to identify his Yang to your Yin.

You might probably be wondering whether or not it is true that opposites tend to attract. Why don't you sit back and take a look at all your past relationships for answering this question? Think about how different you are from others and identify the differences that kept you both perfectly balanced. This will also help you in analyzing your future relationships.

My partner is my beloved

Tantra is all about sacred love, something that goes beyond physical lust. It is about honoring and cherishing your partner while making love. You will have to shower your partner with the same unconditional love that you expect of your partner in return. While communicating with your partner, make use of loving words like 'darling' 'sweetheart' or some other variation of these. These little endearments go a long way when it comes to arousing the feelings of love in them. Calling out your partner with these endearments in public might sound a little strange, but this is the simplest way in which you will be able to communicate your love to your partner.

You feel empowered to say what you want!

When you start feeling empowered, only then will you be able to set boundaries in every aspect of your life, and this includes sex as well. You will discover a newfound sense of self-esteem. The teachings of Tantric sex believe that you are the master of your body and soul. That means you own your body and your soul as well. When your partner shows that he wants to enter you, he will need to seek your permission first. You shouldn't be afraid to speak your mind and say yes or no according to your needs. Open up and say what you enjoy or don't enjoy. Tell your partner about the way that you want to and don't want to be touched. You empower your partner by speaking the truth and will be giving your partner all the information regarding how you like to be pleased.

Chapter 4: Tantric Communication Essentials

Tantric sex places a great deal of importance on the level of communication that exists between two individuals. This is a very invigorating and intimate form of sexual practice and it requires both the individuals to equally contribute both verbally as well as physically for reaping the benefits that this practice has got to offer. While having Tantric sex, it is really important to communicate. Here are a few points that you should keep in mind while doing so.

Looking into the eye

It is critical to maintain eye contact throughout a sexual session. You will have to let go of all your inhibitions and gaze into each other's eyes. It is a common belief in Tantra that the left is considered to be the looking eye and the right eye is considered to be the receiving eye. This means that you will have to concentrate on your partner's right eye while you are talking to him/her. You and your partner should align your bodies in such a manner that there's a free flow of speech and you are also able to maintain eye contact. Don't close your eyes while your partner is talking to you and make a mental note of the different emotions that are emoted while communicating. Eyes are considered to be the mirrors of one's soul. Gaze into your partner's eyes and let them gaze into yours. There are no pretenses; eyes never lie.

Smile

Don't make any funny faces or don't look disinterested while speaking. Have a smile on your face or just a pleasant expression on your face when you are speaking during sex. When you establish a certain bond with your partner, your facial expression will immediately turn more pleasant.

Speaking your mind out

You will need to say out loud what you are thinking. You don't have to hold back or onto your thoughts and don't wait for the right opportunity. Tell your partner everything that you are thinking. If you like something, then communicate your happiness, and your dislike or displeasure if you don't like something. Speaking freely will allow your partner to get an insight into how you think and what you feel. Your mind should be able to freely express what your heart feels.

Emote

Make use of your hands to make gestures while talking. Gestures help in adding onto your speech. Make different signs and symbols to show your partner your appreciation for what they are doing. Make use of your facial expression to convey what you are saying. Use them in addition to your speech and gestures. Don't be afraid to laugh freely, cry, smile or anything else while you are talking to your partner. This will help in becoming more empathetic towards your partner. There are specific hand mudras that can be made use of for channeling your energy and this will allow you to emote in a better manner. Avoid doing certain things that can be quite a turn-off, like cracking your knuckles or grinding your teeth. Instead, concentrate on gazing into your partner's eyes.

Encourage and evoke

When you are speaking to your partner, make sure that you are encouraging him/her to speak up as well. It needs to be mutual, and you will have to make sure that communication is a two-way street. Say things that you know will elicit a response and don't keep on talking continuously. Give your partner some time to respond as well. Provide your partner with an opportunity to express his/her feelings and what he/she is thinking.

Clarity

While talking to your partner before, during or after sex, make sure that you are clear. Modulate your voice accordingly and make sure that you are clear and audible. No one likes it one someone mumbles. It is really important to know what you want to say it and the manner in which you say this matter as well. Put some thought into what you are saying and say it in a proper manner. Simply whispering "I love you" or "you look good" into your partner's ears can be quite a turn on.

Fluidity

Your speech has to be fluid, and you cannot keep pausing in between sentences to say what you are thinking and what you want. When it comes to Tantric sex, each session can last as long as you want it to. Therefore, you need to be prepared both emotionally as well as mentally to say all that you want to. Make sure that you don't tire yourself out by talking too much and channel your thoughts and emotions in a proper manner. Allow this energy to flow freely through your body, and this is the only way in which you can communicate fully with your partner.

Honesty

Don't be afraid and speak honestly. Speak your mind out, and you don't have to exaggerate or lie about something to make it sound nice. Keep it very simple and be truthful about it, if you really want to express yourself freely.

Breathing

Start and concentrate on your breathing and time your breaths so that you can sync them with that of your partner. You don't have to speak constantly; this will simply slow down your breathing. Be aware of how you are breathing and have a good grip on it. Synchronized breathing can be quite a wonderful experience. Breathing can also help your movements while you are performing tantric sex because it makes you more powerful.

Chapter 5: Spin your Chakras and Breathe to Ecstasy

Various practices have been mentioned in this book that will help you in understanding what Tantric sex is all about. These practices make use of different sounds, symbols and sights that will help you along your way to achieving ecstasy. A few techniques have been mentioned in this chapter. You will need to put some time and effort for practicing these techniques and perfect them. One of the most important aspects of tantric sex is the one thing that you are doing right now, breathing. It is crucial that you are breathing properly to ensure that you can attain the deepest possible level of intimacy and the highest level of pleasure that you can experience.

Why is your breath important?
When you are breathing in a proper manner, you are supplying your body with the much-needed oxygen. While you are breathing this also allows for the free movement of sensuality as well as emotions in your body. This will help you in achieving multiple orgasms. Yes, you read it right.

Multiple orgasms! Your breath is the major factor that helps in building your stamina and help you to last longer while having sex. It will also help in making sure that the love that exists between you and your partner stays intimate. This sounds too easy, doesn't it? Well, there's one problem that you need to be addressed in this respect. Now, you are holding your breath too much! Every human being tends to do this. Focus on your breathing pattern at this particular moment. You aren't expanding your chest, are you? Is your breathing shallow? Well, this isn't healthy. In this section, you will learn about three really simply breathing techniques that will help you breathe as you are supposed to.

Focus on the source of your breathing
Have you ever tried to identify the particular place in your body from where your breathing starts? Do you think it starts from your throat, chest or the area around your stomach? Well, it isn't supposed to start from any of these areas. You will need to make a conscious effort to make sure that your breath starts from somewhere deeper in the body. To make sure that you are breathing deeply, take a deep breath and then slowly trace the path of your breath with the help of your hand. Relax, and then exhale. The next time you are taking a deep breath, make sure that it is starting from somewhere as low as your genitals. This will help in making sure that you have got sufficient energy to keep you going while having sex.

Egg to Eagle Exercise
This is a really good technique to make use of, especially while you are sitting. You will need to curl up in a ball and while you are bending, you will have to exhale your breath

swiftly. Now, bring your hands closer to your body, and then place them on the back of your head. Do you feel like your back is stretching? Inhale and then slowly move into a sitting position. Stretch your hands as far away from your body as you can and make sure that your elbows are bent behind your back. Arch your back slowly and push our chest out. This moment will make all the air come rushing back into your chest. Continue with this exercise. Your breathing will be more even after a few repetitions of this exercise.

The wells exercise

The main aim of this particular exercise is to take as much air as you can into your lungs. It is about filling your lungs up with oxygen. This can only be done if you start thinking of your lungs as wells that can be filled up. You will need to work towards increasing the virtual capacity of your lungs. For doing this, keep your arms by your side, and sit in a comfortable place. Once you have inhaled, fill your lungs with as much air as you can, then hold onto this for a few seconds and then exhale all this air from your lungs with some force. It should sound like a gust of wind rushing out of your body. Suck in more air, making as much noise as you can. This will help you in controlling your breathing as well as regulating the sounds that you make while engaged in sex.

The importance of breathing in Tantric sex cannot be stressed enough. Every time you feel that you are inching closer to an impending orgasm, take a few deep breaths and refocus your attention on enjoying the moment, instead of thinking about the orgasm. Enjoy and savor every moment.

Chapter 6: Identify and Worship the God or Goddess Within You

Most people follow the path of Tantra to approach God. God has blessed every aspect of your life; this applies to sex as well. You will be able to connect with God and the divinity, only when you are making love to your partner, since this is the only way in which you are respecting as well as experiencing the divinity that resides within the human body. The teaching of Tantra firmly states that there lies a God in every man and a Goddess in every woman. This implies that your body is the vessel for divinity. For attaining the significant levels of wisdom that are accessible to you, you will simply have to let go of this shell. Your self-esteem will improve when your partner is honoring you, and you are honoring them in return. Only when you can see this aspect of yourself, only then will you be able to see the divinity that lives in others as well clearly.

In this chapter, you will learn and identify the divinity that lives within you. You will be able to identify the God and Goddess within your body and that of your partner as well. This forms the essence of Tantric sex. You will also be able to

33

start to become more enlightened. This chapter covers information about different Gods and Goddesses that are popular in Tantric teachings.

The terms 'God' and 'Goddess'

As mentioned, the teachings of Tantra state that every man and woman should be treated like a God or a Goddess. This is to make sure that you not only think of yourself as a vessel for divinity but treat your partner with the same regard as well. In this manner, you will be able to respect and honor your partner in the manner that you are supposed to. This will also ensure that you can honor the power that exists within the universe.

The different deities usually worshiped in Tantric sex are considered to be beings filled with light. They symbolize various energies as well as relationships. The other terms that are usually used for gods and goddesses are Deva and Devi, priest and priestess, and Daka and Dakini respectively. These deities are believed to possess power and wisdom. This power of theirs can also be projected within your body. This projection simply depends on the various virtues and qualities that you possess.

Goddess is a term that has repeatedly been used in Tantra. It is made use of for describing a woman who is in touch with the feminine power that resides within her body. The initial meaning of this word usually meant a woman who was nurturing and strong. A man is not referred to as God because God is considered to be a superior being in various religions. There are some religions and even a few practices that believe that a person can become a god or a goddess by changing a few aspects of themselves. However, the teachings of Tantric sex state that a person has a certain level of divinity that is present within them since birth and nothing can be done to change this.

Tantric sex rules state that regardless of race, religion or even caste of the person, there's some divinity present in everyone. By referring to a woman as a goddess, you are simply honoring her feminine characteristics that make her a lover, a hunter, seductress and nurturing individual. Only when a woman comes to terms with her characteristics and accepts herself for who she is, will she be able to honor herself and be honored by those around her. By addressing a man as a god, you are simply honoring his basic characteristics of being a protector, healer, provider and a symbol of power. He will need to accept these characteristics that exist within him and only then can his partner honor him. You might be aware of these characteristics, or they might simply be present within you, and you haven't discovered them yet.

Identify your roles and characteristics

When you are getting started with the journey towards Tantric sex, then the first thing that you will need to do is identify the gods or the goddesses that define you. For doing this, you will need to identify your basic characteristics and the different roles that you play in your life. Do you consider yourself to be beautiful? Are you intelligent? Are you an entrepreneur? Are you powerful? And so on, and so forth. You can write down all your answers to such questions. For making things easier for yourself, you can create a collage, or you can use mind-mapping as well. Place a picture of yourself in the center of a sheet and then start writing about all the characteristics that you think you possess.

Once you have gathered information about the various gods and goddesses that has been provided in the latter part of this chapter, you can list down the names of deities that you associate yourself. For instance, if you have written that you are powerful, then perhaps you can relate yourself to Shiva or even Ares. If you think you are beautiful, then you can write down the name of Aphrodite.

Look beyond the superficial layer

You probably will have heard the phrase "never judge a book by its cover." Everyone has probably heard this phrase at one point in time or another. We tend to judge a person solely based on their looks, the way they dress, or even the job that they do. You might have made statements like "she is too skinny," or "he is too short." You probably looked at a person's bank account before agreeing to go out on a date with him. However, Tantra deals with an individual's persona and not their superficial characteristics. There are three basic steps that you will need to follow to worship the divinity that exists within your partner.

The first step would be to accept that there is divinity that exists within you. The second step is to embrace and identify the divinity that exists within your partner as well. You will need to strike a balance between the masculine and the feminine energies of the deities. The third step would be to unite these deities within you, through your union with your partner. This will help in creating the much-needed balance between the two and help you attain a greater level of ecstasy.

Why is it important to worship each other?

Every person is happier when they know that they are being acknowledged. It feels great when you are appreciated by those who are around you. Do you know how you feel when someone notices you? When someone tries to understand you? Tantric sex is all about worshiping yourself and your partner as well. This doesn't mean that you will have to worship each other blindly. It simply means that you both need to shower each other with unconditional love. Unconditional love doesn't mean unconditional power over one another. It simply means that serving each other to the best of your abilities to attain mutual pleasure.

When you start following the path of Tantric sex, you will find that it feels good to hear positive things about yourself and you will also want to keep complimenting your partner. This is the meaning of being worshiped and worshipping your partner.

Learning about the Gods and Goddesses

There are different male and female gods as well as goddesses found in different cultures around the world like Egyptian, Greek, Roman and Indian as well. These gods and goddesses are mostly from an ancient era. Let us learn more about the different goddesses.
Most of the goddesses often represent fertility and life. However, they are also seen as seductresses who seduce their partners and engage in sexual intercourse with them. In this

section, you will read about a few main goddesses, and you can perhaps find a few traits that you associate yourself with.

Aphrodite:

Aphrodite is considered to be the most famous of Greek goddesses. She represents beauty, desire, love and sexuality. She also represents friendship. Aphrodite is often represented by doves, roses, puppies and even dolphins as well. According to Roman mythology, she is referred to as Venus. In Roman mythology, she is the symbol of purity.

Artemis:

She is considered to be the Goddess of hunting. Artemis is a Greek goddess, and she represents the moon and is a virgin goddess. She is a warrior and a hunter, the female counterpart to complement Ares, the God of war.

Athena:

The goddess of wisdom and knowledge. She is the patron goddess of Athens. Strategy and planning are the two traits that are commonly associated with Athena.

Juno:

Juno or Hera, depending upon whether it is the Greek or Roman version of mythology is considered to be a mother like figure with a nurturing and a calming nature.

Hindu Goddesses:

There are various goddesses in India and Nepal, and each of them has been given a lot of importance. Various ceremonies are conducted to honor each of these goddesses. The main goddesses are mentioned here.

Durga is considered to be the mother of all goddesses. Tara is considered to represent wisdom as well as kindness. Lakshmi is the goddess of wealth and prosperity. Saraswati is the goddess of various art forms and skill. Kali represents strength and power. She is also the protector of the realm.

Gods from Different Cultures

Every religion has different gods and goddesses. These gods often have a counterpart in the form of a goddess. There are different deities worshiped by different cultures. They all represent immense strength, power, and are often thought of as super beings. This section covers carious gods from different religions. You might be able to identify your traits or those of your partner in this list given here.

Hindu Gods:

Hindu gods include Lord Shiva who has got immense power and Lord Vishnu is considered to be the God of all Gods. There are different manifestations of Lord Shiva, and there are quite a few representations of his dark side as well. Shakti is the consort of Lord Shiva. Lord Shiva and Shakti form a powerful pair and represent pure energy. Ganesh is a very popular god as well; he is a young boy with the head of an elephant. Lord Ganesh is known to remove obstacles and spread happiness. Lord Rama and Sita form a couple that is often worshiped all over India, they are considered to be the perfect couple and represent the harmony that should exist between a husband and wife.

Greek gods:

There are numerous Greek gods, and they have all become famous because of the strength and power that they hold.

Zeus is considered to be the greatest of all; he is the King of all gods and the supremely powerful Alpha-male. Eros is commonly referred to, as Cupid, and he is cherub or a little boy who is often mischievous and often keeps shooting arrows of love at people around him. He is the God of love. Dionysus is the Greek and the Roman god of lust. According to the legends, he always chased women and indulged in drinking a lot of wine. He indeed is the god of lust.

Chapter 7: Prepare Your Body

The teachings of Tantric sex believe that your body is a temple of love and that it is really important that you keep in healthy. If you want to achieve higher levels of ecstasy, then you will need to keep fit. In this chapter, you will learn about the different tips that you can make use of for keeping your body fit and healthy. There are specific yoga positions that you can make use of if you want to facilitate the movement of energy in your body. The practices that have been mentioned in this chapter are helpful in helping you in channeling as well as controlling sexual energy in your body.

More often than not, we tend to take our bodies for granted. We don't worry about it, and we don't realize that the body is the bridge that will help you in attaining bliss. You will need to worship your body and treat it with the care and love it deserves if you want to attain a higher level of bliss.

Building love for your body through the looking glass

One of the most important things that you will need to do while you are preparing your body for Tantric sex is to let go of all the different negative thoughts that you might harbor about your body. You will have to view every part of your body, including your genitals and see whether or not they are healthy. If you feel that you are fat, simply tell yourself that you are curvy. You must do this regularly to make sure that you let go of any negative feelings that you might have towards your body and instead enjoy yourself and have fun while having sex.

When was the last time you have seen yourself naked? Try standing naked in front of a full-length mirror. You can do this after taking a shower if you prefer to do this. Take a close look at every inch of your body. Start from your feet right up to the top of your head. If you notice that you are criticizing yourself, then stop then and there and instead give yourself a compliment. Replace every negative thought with a positive one. If you feel that your ass is fat or that your thighs are thick, simply think that you have a luscious figure! You needn't worry about what you look like. Change every negative feeling into a positive one. Then observe your genitals. You should focus on every little aspect of your genitals, the colors, shape and also the moistness in particular areas. It is really important that you do this to be confident about your body.

You can observe your first chakra, the base chakra that is located at the end of your spine and the anal region. This chakra provides you with the idea of security, and you need to take some time and observe this area in the same manner in which you observed your genitals. Use two mirrors if you need to.

The connection between yoga and tantric sex

Yoga is perhaps one of the best ways in which you will be able to prepare your body for Tantric sex. Yoga and Tantric sex are closely related. Therefore, it wouldn't come as a surprise that most of the Tantric masters have also mastered the art of yoga. Learning yoga will help in gaining control over their bodies. Practicing yoga will also help you in gaining control over your mind and body. It will also help in controlling your body movements. Gaining control over your body will let you experience multiple orgasms and also have control over your ejaculation. This will have a positive effect on your health and your sex life as well.

Simple yoga movements

This section will help you learn a few basic yoga poses that you can perform to improve your overall health and stamina. In the next section, you will learn about the different tantric exercises that you can, and your partner can perform together. This will help in increasing your intimacy and comfort level with each other.

The Head lift

Make sure that you are standing up straight for this. Then tilt your head upward and tilt it in such a manner that string from the sky was pulling it upwards. Keep your mouth closed, and you will need to inhale through your nose. When you are inhaling, make sure that you are moving your shoulder blades backward so that it looks like they are trying to touch each other. It should feel like your feet are fixed to the ground. Relax your stance and then repeat this process.

The Cobra pose

You can lie down on the floor or a yoga mat. Now extend your body to make sure that your stomach is touching the floor. Then place your hands under your shoulders so that your elbows are placed at the back. Lift your chest off the floor and tilt your head so that it looks like a curve. Make sure that you are looking upwards. This pose should like a cobra that's about to strike. Relax your stance and then repeat this process.

The Cat pose

Once you are done with the Cobra pose, you will have to gently lower your head and slowly rise up on your knees. This should look like you are crouching, so stretch your spine in the opposite direction than what you did in the Cobra pose.

The Resting pose

Once you have finished the Cat pose, you will have to assume the Cobra pose. Stretch your arms outwards. Breathe in deeply and freely. Make sure that your forehead is resting on the ground and that your chest is touching your knees.

Tantric exercises

If you want to add some leverage to your practice of Tantric sex, then you can start practicing a few exercises and breathing techniques that will help you in making your sexual experience even better. These exercises, as well as breathing techniques, are best suited when done with your partner, but they can be done on your own as well. These exercises and breathing techniques have been mentioned in this section.

Shoulder stand

Shoulder stands are helpful for women for assuming the various Tantric poses with ease, but then again men can practice them as well. For performing a simple shoulder pose, the person will have to lie down flat on a mat or even the floor with his/her legs stretched straight and their hands resting by their side. The person will then have to lift the legs at a 90-degree angle so that their upper torso remains glued to the floor. Their legs should be lifted a little higher than their lower back, and their hands should be placed on their back for supporting this posture. Practicing this technique will help in developing the much-needed flexibility for assuming various Tantric sex positions.

Boat pose

This pose is once again helpful for women. The individual performing this pose should sit with a straight back, and their legs should be stretched out. Then the individual will have to lift their legs at a 45-degree angle and then stretch their hands outwards so that their fingers are pointing towards their feet. Try and maintain this pose for three minutes and then relax. Repeat this pose five times.

Three legged dog pose

This pose is helpful for stretching the hamstring muscles, and these are quite often made use of in Tantric sex. For performing this pose, the person must lie down on their stomach on a mat while their hands are placed on their sides. Your palms should be placed next to the chest and support your feet with your toes. Lift your body in such a manner that your toes support your body weight. This position should seem like your body is creating a triangle, with the floor forming the base of the triangle. The right leg must then be slowly lifted upwards. Lift your leg as far as your body would permit. Then return to neutral position and repeat the same with the other leg.

Bridge pose

This is a pose that's suitable for both the sexes. For performing this technique, you will need to lie down on your back and then bend your legs in such a manner so that your knees are pointing upwards. Your feet should be placed close to your bum. The lower torso should be lifted, and your hands should lie on either side of your body for providing support. Repeat this five times.

Kegels

This pose will help women in strengthening their pelvic muscles. This helps in tightening the grip of the pelvic muscles and for making the vaginal passage seem tighter, thereby making it a far more stimulating experience for both parties. For performing this exercise, the woman will have to concentrate on the vaginal muscles and pull them in and release. The suction can be held onto for as long as possible and then released. This exercise can be done anywhere and at any point of time. It also helps muscle control considerably.

Kapalbhatti

This is an easy breathing technique, and the man can perform this right before his orgasm. This can also be performed every morning for better results. For performing this technique, you will simply have to take several short and sharp breaths. It is best to do this while sitting upright with your legs crisscrossed. The focus of this exercise is more on the exhalation of air than inhalation. The mouth should be closed while exhaling and this should create a loud sound while letting the air out. Perform this in sets of 3.

Pranayama

This is another exercise that can be performed by both the sexes and it helps in assisting and controlling your breathing during Tantric sex. For performing this technique, the person can sit upright in the lotus pose and place the right thumb on their right nostril and point a finger at the center of your forehead. Breath in through your left nostril, hold the breath for a few seconds and then release it through your right nostril. While doing this, the right nostril should be freed, and the left nostril should be pressed up. Repeat this five times. This can help the energy levels to increase and also helps awareness.

Chapter 8: Tantric Positions and Techniques

In this chapter, you will learn about different Tantric sex positions and techniques that you can make use of for spicing up your sex life.

The Sidewinder

This position is inspired from the yoga position of the same name, and this technique allows for deep penetration. It also provides for the couple to maintain eye contact. For performing this technique, the woman will have to lie down on her side and supports the weight of her upper body with the help of her hands. She will have to lift one of her legs and place it on her lover's shoulder while the other leg is lying on the bed. A variation of this same position is that alternatively the man can lie down behind the woman and enter his partner from behind.

The Yab Yum

The Yab Yum position is considered to be one of the best positions for having tantric sex. It is a fairly easy position to perform, and it allows for simultaneous orgasms. This position does help in stimulating all the right spots. Also, the man's hands happen to be free in this position, and he can touch his lover's body as he pleases, and since the couple would be facing each other, it allows for passionate kisses as well. The man will have to sit cross-legged on the bed or any other comfortable surface and keep his back straight. The woman will have to straddle him and wrap her legs around his lower back. It allows for slow up and down movements that can help the couple in achieving a well-timed orgasm.

The padlock

This pose allows the man to get a good look at his lover's face and vice versa. This is a very sexy pose and helps in pleasuring both the partners. For performing this technique, the woman will have to be seated on a high platform like a table or even the kitchen counter. She will then have to lean back and balance her upper torso and her head with the help of her hands by leaning onto her elbows. The man will have to stand between her parted legs and enter her. This is one pose that doesn't have to be restricted to the bedroom and is perfect for an impromptu romp.

The butterfly

This technique is believed to give both the partners a chance to attain a high level of ecstasy and allows for deep penetration. For performing this technique, the girl will have to lie down on the table in such a way that her butt lies at the edge of the table and the man will need to help lift her lower back slightly off the table and then place both her legs over his shoulders. Her vagina would be free for him to penetrate while standing in between her legs. Since her legs are closed together, this tightens the vaginal canal and provides a tight fit. The man will have to enter her while her butt is in mid air.

The double-decker

This is an extremely erotic pose and will help in achieving an orgasm easily. The man will also be provided with a good view of all the action that is going on down there, and his hands will also have unrestricted access to lay with his lover's butt. This position is quite empowering for women since they have all the control here. For performing this technique, the man will have to sit on the bed while his legs are folded under his body. The woman will then have to face away from him and place her feet one either side of her lover while her feet are placed flat on the surface to provide her with some support. Once she has lowered herself onto his erect penis, then she will simply have to start moving forwards and backward or can even opt for an up and down motion. The man will have to simply sit back and enjoy the show.

The hot seat

This is a great pose since it allows both the parties to have the same amount of control and exude the same amount of pressure for having a wonderful sexual experience. Men and women will have equal footing in this particular position. For performing this pose, the man will have to sit on the bed and support his upper body with his knees. He will then have to move the lower part of his legs backward and place them slightly apart. The woman will then have to assume the same position but she will do so while facing away from him and her butt would be pressing against his scrotum and her back against his chest. Her legs would be joined and then placed in the space that is available between his legs and the man will have to penetrate her from behind. For this position to be effective, both the partners will have to stay as close to each other as possible.

Row boat

This position is a slight modification of the woman on top position. In this pose, the bodies will have to be positioned in such a way that both the partners will get to have a good look at each other's face while engaged in the act. For performing this, the man will have to sit down on a chair that can slightly bend backward. The woman will then have to place herself on his lap and then place her legs on either side of the chair. The girl will have to start an up and down movement by herself, or her partner can help her by placing his hand under her bum and helping her move in an upwards and downwards manner.

The mermaid

This is a slightly varied version of the butterfly, and it allows for a more comfort and better grip. In this pose, the man can play with his lover's feet. Don't forget that feet are considered to be one of the most sensitive and erogenous parts of a woman's body. For performing this technique, the woman will have to assume the same position as she did in the butterfly, but her butt should be propped with the help of a pillow. Her legs will have to stretch out and should be at a 90-degree angle. The man will have to stand close to the table and penetrate her.

Tidal wave

This pose is quite comfortable, and it is an erotic treat. This will blow your mind. This pose is a slight modification of the classic missionary style. In this position, the woman will have to assume the role that a man usually does in the missionary style. For performing this, the man will have to lie down flat on his back, and his arms will have to be placed by his side. The woman will have to lie on top of him, and the man will have to insert his penis into her vagina. The woman will have to completely stretch out her legs so that they are resting atop his. Her palms should be placed on his forearm for providing her some support. The woman will then have to start moving her pelvis in an upward and downward movement.

Lap dance

This is a really good pose for a man to experience his lover's body in all its glory. His hands will be free to roam around her body, and he can do what he wants. The woman will be facing way from him as she would have, had she been giving him a lap dance. For performing this pose, the man will have to sit down on a chair, and his back will need to be kept straight. The woman will then sit on his lap and balance herself by placing her hands on his upper thighs or even his stomach. She will then have to lift herself slowly and place the backs of her calves and lowers herself onto his penis. Another variation of this would be that the woman will have to lower herself onto his penis while facing her lover and this will give him quite a good view of her breasts. He can decide to tease and play with them for as long as he pleases.

Pretzel

This is another pose that is pleasing to look at and even very easy to assume. This will make the couple feel extremely sexy. For performing this technique, the couple will have to kneel in front of each other. The man will have to move forwards, and the woman will wrap her arms around him. The woman will then lift herself up and place her left leg next to her lover's right foot; her foot will be facing downwards. The man will then have to place his left leg near her right foot. When looked at a couple engaged in this pose, they resemble a pretzel, a very sexy and appetizing pretzel.

The spread

This is a very basic and an extremely sexy position. This allows the woman to obtain great pleasure because it lets her caress her lover and allows him the access to pleasure her. For performing this technique, the woman will have to sit at the very edge of the sofa or even the bed and spread her legs apart. The man will then have to stand in between her legs and penetrate her. She can move closer to him and kiss him while his hands have got the access to her full body.

The intertwine

This pose does look tough and nearly impossible to mimic, but then it can be pleasurable if it's done properly. This pose is aesthetically appealing. For performing this technique, the couple will have to sit close to each other and face one another. The man will have to place his legs on either side of his partner. The woman will then have to lift both of her legs and place them on either side of her lover's sides, under his arms. The man's upper arms will lock the woman's legs in place, and the woman will then have to lift her upper arms and place them above his elbows. The man will then lift his legs and place them on top of her hands. This does sound quite complicated, doesn't it? Well, all the effort that goes into it will be worth your while.

The G-force

This is perhaps one of the hottest tantric sex poses there is. This is the piece de resistance of all sex poses. The man has got complete control over his lover in this pose, but both the individuals involved will derive extreme pleasure from this pose. For performing this position, the woman will have to lie down on her back on the bed, and the man must kneel by her legs. He will then slowly lift her torso off the bed so that she's balancing herself with her head and her shoulders placed on the bed. The man can either stretch her legs at a 90-degree angle or penetrate her, or he can also pull them apart and place her feet just below his chest and enter her.

The waterfall

In this pose, the woman will have to place her hand on her lover's penis and then let her fingertips brush his scrotum very slowly and gently. It is a good idea to make use of some lubricant for making it more pleasurable. Her hands need to be placed on either side of his testicles, and then she will have to slowly slide her hands up till they reach the sensitive tip of his penis. Once this is done, the woman should give the man a while to cool down, and he will then have to reciprocate the service he received. The man has to cup his lover's vagina and touch all her sensitive spots. He should slide his hands over her clitoris and her vaginal outer lips.

The serpent

For this, the woman will have to slowly stretch the shaft of her lover's penis with one of her hands and let the other hand trace small circles right under the head of the shaft. This is similar to giving a slow and gentle hand job. Continue these motions in a clockwise direction and then once you reach the head of the penis shift to anticlockwise direction. Keep this up for as long as your lover can endure it.

Tantric triangle of touch

The woman will have to lie down on her back and spread her legs slightly and bend them at the knee. The man will then have to insert his index and middle finger into her vagina and slightly curl them upwards till they make a come here movement. This will provide the perfect stimulation for her

G-Spot. This will make her moan in pleasure. While doing this, he should place the palm of his other hand on her lower abdomen and apply a little pleasure. This combined stimulation will quickly push her off the edge.

The seesaw

There is nothing remotely innocent about this particular seesaw. This is very erotic. The woman will have to lie down on her back on the bed, and her pelvis needs to be slightly tilted upwards. A pillow can be propped under her pelvis for doing so. The man will then have to lift her feet and gently fold them so that her knees are resting on her breasts and the soles of her feet are touching his chest. This position allows unrestricted access to a woman's vagina, and the upward tilt will ensure that he hits her G-Spot every time he thrusts into her.

Tub Tangle

Get your man to recline in a tub that's filled with water and the woman will have to straddle him while her back is facing him. Once his penis has penetrated her, he will have to sit up so that you both are facing each other. Then she will have to wrap her legs around him, and he will do the same so that their elbows are under their partner's knees. Hold onto each other as tightly as you can and start a swaying back and forth motion. This does allow for some passionate kissing.

Love Triangle

The woman will have to lie down on her back on the floor or the bed and then she will need to lift her left leg up into the air. Her right legs should be stretched out to her right side, such that both her legs are lying perpendicular to each other. She will then have to move her right hand and clasp her right knee and form a triangle on the bed with the use of her right leg and her right hand. The man will need to crouch a little and enter her while holding her knee. This position would give the man better pelvic control and also the opportunity of touching in as many ways as you would want to. A slight variation can be added to this pose by asking the man to rotate his hips in a circular motion while thrusting into the woman; this will push the couple to their brink.

Now and Zen

This pose can be made use of for providing a moment of respite from the impending climax. Tantric sex isn't about finding quick release; it is about savoring the moment. What better way to do so, than to control yourself right before reaching the point of no return. When you feel that either you or your partner is close to climaxing, take a few seconds and break free of the position that you both are in. The man can simply roll onto his side and stay inside his partner all the while. This position simply asks for a moment of respite. Slow thrusting is permissible, but if you feel that, you are about to climax, then take a moment, pause, perhaps enjoy a little bit of kissing and touching before continuing where you had let go. This position provides the much-needed intimacy during the sexual intercourse to make the whole experience more loving and wholesome.

Torrid Tug-of-War

The woman will have to sit cross-legged on the floor or any other comfortable surface and then slowly sink onto his erect penis and wrap her legs around his back. This position will allow the couple to be facing each other and this means that you can grab hold of each other's elbows for providing some support and lean into the direction away from your partner. This is like playing a game of coy tug-of-war. If you both happen to be flexible, then one partner can tilt their heads back and lean backward, away from the other partner. This position will allow for the alignment of your bodies, and it will make you connect with your partner. It forms an intimate connection and helps in building momentum. Both the partners get to be equal players in this pose and the penetration can be controlled alternatively by the partners.

The Python

The man will have to lie down in this position, and his legs should be kept close together while his arms are resting by his sides. The woman will have to lower herself onto his penis and mount him slowly. Once the man has penetrated her, then she can stretch herself out above so that she's resting fully on his body. Both of your bodies would be perfectly aligned, and you can grasp each other's hands for building some momentum and also for providing some support. The woman will then have to slowly lift her torso off his so that it almost seems like a snake that's poised to strike. She can push against his feet for adding some more movement. You will both be touching each other fully, and her breasts would be rubbing against his chest, your hands would be grasped tightly, and his thighs would be rubbing against hers. It not only allows for deep penetration, but it also allows for clitoral stimulation. Since the couple would be facing each other, this allows for some passionate kissing as well. All the erogenous zones in the body would be stimulated.

Yes! Yes! Yes!

In this pose, the woman will be lying face down on the mattress, and she will need to scoot forward till her head and her torso are hanging off the side of the bed and she will need to support her upper body with the help of her palms placed on the floor. The man will then need to crawl between her legs and then penetrate her from behind. The man can always hold onto his lover's hips for getting a better leverage. The couple engaged in this position seems like a sideways Y and therefore the name of this position. Well, yes it is quite cheeky. This position is really good for quick in and out movements that will send you both reeling in pleasure. This is an upside down pose that also allows for the blood to go rushing straight to the head. This position can be slightly tricky and exhausting as well and therefore you might not be able to keep at it all night long. However, it does add a distinct exotic flavor to your regular romps and spice things up. A slight variation that can be added to this pose is that the woman can add some grinding motion to this position to allow for dual stimulation.

X Marks the Spot

In this pose, the woman has got to lie down on the bed or any other soft surface of choice with her head propped on a pillow. She will have to bring her knees up to her chest and cross her legs at her ankles. The man will then have to kneel in front of her and slowly lean in a while pulling her hips towards his groin. She will have to keep her thighs pressed together while he starts thrusting into her. This will allow for a back and forth motion and the crossing and clamping of legs will simply add some more friction. If the woman can start contracting her PC muscles, it will become even more pleasurable.

Time Bomb

The man will have to sit down on a low chair with his legs in a relaxed position. While facing away from him, the woman will have to straddle him and place her feet on the floor while slowly lowering onto his penis. Her knees will have to be bent at a 90-degree angle. She will have to place herself at the tip of his penis, and then he will have to thrust into her. It is quite an affectionate pose and allows for maximum contact between the partners. Women will assume all the control in this pose and men have got the chance to wrap their arms around their lover's body and explore it to their heart's content. He can also stimulate her clitoris for her added pleasure.

Arc de Triomphe

This is quite a sexy pose. The man will have to sit down on the bed with his legs stretched in front of him. His lover will have to crawl up to him and then straddle his erect member. Once you both are comfortable in this position, she will have to arch her back as much as she can. Being flexible will come in handy in this particular pose. Women need to be careful while doing this because the unnecessary strain on their lower back can have serious repercussions. She can gently ease back and reach back to hold her ankles. Now, the real fun begins. The man will have to lean forward and start thrusting into her. Women will have to brace themselves for the onslaught of movement by holding onto their ankles. The man will get to enjoy the panoramic view of his lover's body and feast on it. If the man wishes so, he can lean down and kiss her chest as well.

Head Game

In this pose, the woman will need to lie down on the ground or any other flat surface while her face is facing upwards. Her hands will have to support her lower body; she will then have to lift her legs up, and her back as well so that they are lying perpendicular to the ground. She can support her weight by propping up her arms against her lower back. While she is holding onto her ankles, the man will need to kneel before her and bring his knees towards her shoulders. He can always hold onto her hips so that it will keep them both steady and she can hold onto his thighs for some extra support. This is upside down action, make sure that you are gentle with your lover and it can be quite tricky to get it right in the first go itself. Women, all those Kegels that you have been practicing can be put to some good use in this position. For making it more pleasurable, start contracting your PC muscles and start milking your lover's penis.

Supernova

This is a pose that pretty much starts out by looking like a regular cowgirl position. Instead of the woman mounting him lengthwise, she will have to mount him while lying perpendicular to him on the bed. When she senses her man approaching a climax, she can gently grind on his torso and lean on her knees and keep on inching forward towards the edge of the bed so that his head and shoulders are hanging off the side of the bed. Now, she can resume her ride once again. This position places all the control with the woman, and she can ride her man, however, she pleases. It also allows for deeper penetration, and since all the blood would rush to the man's head in this pose, he will experience a spectacular orgasm. It is quite empowering to the Goddess to see that she's got the reigns in this pose. Aesthetically, it is quite a sight for the man to behold.

Love Seat

The man will need to lie down on his back and prop his head with the help of a few pillows and spread his legs slightly. The woman will have to lower herself onto his erect penis while facing away from him. It does resemble the reverse cowgirl position. She will need to place her feet between his legs on either side of the floor or the bed that he's lying on.

Her right-hand needs to be placed on the right side of his hip and the left one on the left side. By using this for support, she can slowly lower herself onto his penis. The woman's hands and feet will let her control the motion, and she can set the pace. The man just needs to lie down and enjoy the work that his partner is doing. His hands are free to roam her body. Well, the inner goddess will be happy and will relish the control that's been placed in her hands.

Bed Spread

The woman will have to bend over her side so that her breasts are resting gently on the mattress and her feet are hanging on the floor. The man will then have to move behind her and enter her from behind. While doing this, he can hold or lift her legs slightly so that it allows for better penetration and also gives him the necessary leverage for thrusting as he would like to. Since the woman's legs have been lifted off the floor, all that she needs to do is let the guy do all the work and enjoy his efforts. This position gives all the control to the man, and he is in charge of the depth and the speed of movements.

Chapter 9: Tantric Sex and Men's Multiple Orgasms

One of the most important aspects of Tantric sex is that it differentiates between climaxing during sex and ejaculating. If you feel that you aren't fully satisfied even after having ejaculating, that's because you might not have experienced an orgasm. Therefore, it is not necessary for a man to ejaculate to have an orgasm. By making use of the different methods of controlling an orgasm that has been mentioned in the philosophy of Tantra, you will be able to experience multiple orgasms and orgasms that will last for longer than the ones that you are usually used to. Doesn't this sound fantastic? Who said women alone are capable of experiencing multiple orgasms?

There's a particular Tantric technique that you can make use of, and it will allow you to have multiple orgasms. However, before getting yourself acquainted with this particular level of sexual prowess, you will need to achieve control over your orgasms. There are three different strategies that you can make use of for gaining control over your orgasms.

Get ready to Kegel

The pubic muscles that are present in your groin are the muscles that are responsible for controlling your sex. These muscles are the same ones that you make use of for controlling your urge to pee. Strengthening these pubic muscles will allow you to have a certain degree of control over your orgasm, and an efficient way in which you can do this is by practicing Kegels. Kegels are an extremely simple and easy exercise. These can be pretty much performed anywhere and at any time. In this exercise, you will simply need to clench and release your pubic muscles. Repeat this around two dozen times, either before or after you has had your meals. Don't go overboard with this particular exercise. After you have been practicing this for two weeks, you can increase the duration of holding onto the squeeze from about two or three seconds to about ten seconds. This will help you in holding off your climax.

Keep your cool

This might sound strange, but the best way in which you can prolong your intercourse is by keeping your cool. If you feel that your orgasm is fast approaching, and then you will simply have to calm down, slow down your breathing and your thrusting motions as well. Keep in mind that this might also lead to some awkwardness with your partner if you don't communicate about it. Don't feel awkward and tell your partner your reason for slowing down.

Take it slow

When you start having sex with your partner, make sure that you are taking things slowly during the initial stage. The slower the sex is, the more intense your orgasm would be because of all the buildup. Make sure that your breathing is regular and when you feel that, your climax is approaching; follow the steps mentioned in the previous points. Calm yourself, slow down your breathing, and clench your pelvic muscles.

Once you feel that your orgasm is subsiding, and then you can resume your thrusting motion once again. Keep repeating this process for as long as you can hold off. Build your excitement and keep on going. This buildup will make your orgasm last longer, and it will be more powerful. Once you feel that you are close to orgasm, try and clench your pubic muscles while it is happening. This will not only prevent you from ejaculating, but it will let you experience the pleasure of an orgasm and not lose your erection. This means that you can keep going even after experiencing an orgasm, doesn't that sound good? After a little practice, you will be able to hold off for a while longer and have sex for hours together.

Chapter 10: The Female Orgasm

Tantra not only provides a way to deal with problems that men face during sex, it even addresses the problems that women tend to face while having sex. This is the reason why there are different practices applicable to women in this spiritual way of living. It is a common belief in Tantric philosophy that the most powerful sex organ for a woman is her mind. This means that her sexual arousal is capable of being dampened by her negative thinking and emotions that restrict her lust. These thoughts and emotions can be caused due to anxiety, anger, or even guilt. Regardless of the reason of their origin, these emotions can have a negative effect on the sex drive of a woman. This would make a woman distracted while having sex.

It is crucial to place less importance on the theatrics that are involved in the process of sexual intercourse and more on what the woman is feeling while going through the motions of sex. Here are a few techniques that will help a woman in achieving an orgasm.

Clitoral Stimulation

Most men are usually unaware of the fact that not do only women get turned on or excited by vaginal penetration. There's nothing wrong in not being able to achieve an orgasm through penetration. In fact, it is only a small fraction of women who tend to climax through penetration. Sex, in itself, is quite a stimulating act, but the clitoris is the gem that provides the majority of the sexual pleasure that a woman experiences. Therefore, it is really important to concentrate on the clitoris as well. Men, remember that you will need to be gentle while you are stimulating a woman's clitoris. It is extremely sensitive and being rough would just make your partner feel extreme discomfort. Additionally, the pressure of having to orgasm also tends to take out the fun from the act of sex. So, don't pressure your partner to orgasm.

G-Spot

The teachings of Tantra show that there lies a sacred spot within a woman's vagina that is referred to as the G-Spot and it is extremely sensitive. When stimulated in the desired manner it can produce mind-blowing orgasms. The G-Spot is believed to be located at the top of the vaginal canal, a few inches within the vagina. You can stimulate your partner's G-Spot by gently massaging the top of the vaginal canal. This spot would feel like a slight bump against the smooth vaginal wall. Gently brush it to elicit a reaction from your partner. You will be able to realize when you have found the magic button from your partner's reaction. Majority of women can climax if this sacred spot is stimulated properly. On rare occasions, when stimulated properly, women can ejaculate as well. The G-Spot is also believed to be the resting spot of Kundalini, the dormant sexual energy that is present in women. When stimulated properly, the Kundalini awakens and flows through the body.

Chapter 11: Teachings of Tantric Sex

In this chapter, let us take a closer look at the teachings of Tantric sex that will help in not only improving the level of intimacy but also the sexual pleasure that you and your partner experience. This will have a positive effect on your relationship. When these teachings are made use of in the proper manner, then it will put you a step closer to achieving enlightenment. Each one of these teachings can be made use of in a sexual and a non-sexual way.

Breathe

Remember to keep breathing. You probably would have understood by now the importance of breathing when it comes to Tantric sex. It is not just about tantric sex; any of the teachings that have originated in the East, regarding the attainment of enlightenment, tend to place a great deal of importance on breathing. It is crucial that you understand the reason why this is done and the manner in which it is related to Tantra as well as the spiritual development of an individual.

The answer to this is quite simple, every living thing breathes. We breathe all the time, and if we do stop breathing for prolonged periods of time, it will ultimately result in death or even unconsciousness. In this manner, it could be simply understood that breathing can be related to our state of consciousness. Think of breath as energy. Every breath that we take fills our body with oxygen and takes away carbon dioxide in this process. This oxygen that we inhale is then supplied to different cells in the body. Oxygen and breathing are fundamental for the functioning of our bodies. Breathing isn't a voluntary or conscious function. It is something that our body has been designed to do. You might never pay any attention to the way you are breathing, but you never really stop breathing when you are alive. Isn't it intimidating how our life depends on a function that we don't even do voluntarily?

So, what would happen if you start to make breathing a conscious function instead of an involuntary action? All the teachings that have originated in the East, including the teachings of Tantra, believe that breathing should also be a voluntary action. Like mentioned earlier, breath is energy, and by being able to control your breathing, you will also be able to regulate the movement of energy within your body.

It is quite interesting to note the benefits of conscious and regulated breathing can have on different aspects of your life, including your sex life. It is common that while people are engaged in any sexual activity they tend to hold their breath. Every time you get excited, you might notice that you tend to hold your breath. You probably hold onto your breath without even realizing that you are doing so. When you stop breathing, this will disrupt the flow of energy in your body as well. Making breathing a conscious act while engaged in sex will help you in learning to control your energy and the movement of energy in your body. This teaching of Tantra is all about taking breaths in a relaxed and calm manner. Let your breath flow slowly through your body. If you want to achieve a full body orgasm, then you will have to make sure that your breathing is deep and even. When you start focusing on this, you will realize that you can climax more easily.

Relax

The tension in your muscles and body will act as an obstruction in a manner that is similar to shallow breathing. The muscular tension that you tend to experience when you are engaged in any sexual activity is not a conscious one. One of the principles of Tantric sex is that you will need to be aware of this muscular tension that exists in your body and so that you are aware of all the different muscles that are being held up due to tension. You do require a little bit of tension for facilitating movement in the body and also for holding up the body, but that's it. Muscular tension isn't required in every part of the body.

If you start making the decision of tensing up your muscles a conscious one, then you will notice that you are probably tensing up a few muscles in your body unnecessarily while having sex. For instance, a man might end up tensing all his muscles while receiving oral sex. Whereas he's simply supposed to let go and enjoy the attention being showered by his partner, instead he is tensing up the muscles in his torso and legs. In such a case, all the extra tension is unnecessary, and this simply obstructs the free flow of energy in the body. Focus your attention on relaxing all these tensed muscles. Focus on your breathing and enjoy the sexual warmth that is flowing through your body.

However, it is crucial that relaxation doesn't simply include the letting go of the physical tension, but the mental tension as well. Let go of all the unnecessary thoughts and expectations. Savor the moment, enjoy the warmth, the sensations, and don't hold yourself back.

Sounds that can help

Sounds are crucial when it comes to the movement of energy in the body. Some people may not be comfortable, or they might even be conscious about the sounds that they make when aroused. These considerations shouldn't be taken seriously while engaging in Tantric sex. Let go of all the inhibitions that are holding you back. Express yourself as freely as you want to. There is no restriction apart from the ones that you have imposed on yourself. Make all the sounds that you feel like making. These sounds are involuntary reactions to the pleasure that you are experiencing, and they are connected with the emotions and sensations that you are experiencing. If you are silent or quiet, then the movement of sexual energy in your body gets slow. When you are vocal in expressing what you are feeling, the energy starts to move in the body. Tantric sex is all about awakening the dormant sexual energy that is present within the body and then making use of it for achieving enlightenment. Well, how will the energy move when you are anxious about something as trivial as the way you sound?

You don't have to decipher the different sounds that are associated with the different emotions that you are experiencing. You moan, groan, or take a sharp breath depending upon the pleasure that you are experiencing. All the various sounds that you make contribute to the pleasure that you and your partner would derive from sex. The sounds produced needn't be coherent; it is just the expression of the emotions that you might be experiencing at a particular moment. While you are having sex, there would be a few instances that might make you feel ecstatic, and this will be represented in the sounds that you would make. There might be a few unpleasant experiences as well. You should verbally express your displeasure as well as pleasurable feelings, and you needn't hold yourself back. You need to communicate your pleasure or displeasure to your partner. It is not just about being vocal. You can be verbal in your expression as well. Not just sounds, but words can also be made use of for communicating the same. If you feel that, you are enjoying something that your partner is doing, and then you should communicate the same to them without any inhibitions. This not only provides some encouragement but also lets your partner know that they are doing something right. In the same manner, if you don't like something then you should express your discomfort to your partner. Letting go of your inhibitions is the only way in which you will be able to truly experience unbridled pleasure.

Eye contact is essential

This might sound like an obvious thing. Well, it does enhance the overall sexual experience. Looking at your partner while engaged in any sexual act will make the experience more intense eye contact doesn't mean that you stare wistfully into your partner's eyes. Move over to the longing look a love struck puppy has in its eyes. We are talking about some serious X-rated gazing, so get ready for it.

This will help you attain some extra intimacy. For getting started, you and your partner can find a comfortable spot to sit so that you both will be able to look into each other's eyes. Take a moment to gather your thoughts; usually, a deep breath will do the trick for you. Once you feel that you are ready, you can open your eyes and gaze into your partner's eyes. Allow your partner the access to see you, your true self, sans any pretenses and in a similar manner, you can gaze at them. This might feel a little stupid initially, but it will prove to be quite effective.

Allow yourself to communicate through your eyes and not just your genitals. You can let your eyes wander over each other's body. Let your partner see the lust in your eyes and the wanton abandonment. Nothing would be a better turn on than knowing that your partner desires you and needs you. In the manner, that sounds and touch can communicate, in the same way, you can communicate a lot more by making use of just your eyes alone. This will help you both communicate with each other in an earnest manner.

Pay attention

Energy flows in the body according to your attention. You will need to concentrate on this flow of energy in your body. If you want to experience a full body orgasm, then the energy in your body should spread to every single cell. You will have to start paying some extra attention to the highly sexualized feelings that you want to experience throughout your body. If a woman wants to enjoy a vaginal orgasm, then she will need to focus on prying out the dormant sexual energy that is present within her and coax it to move freely in her body. You can make use of the other principles of Tantra for focusing your attention. For drawing out the energy and directing it towards the spot that you want it to go to, then you will need to visualize the same. Picture this energy moving from its resting place to the place where you want to experience pleasure. The principles of Tantra suggest that energy needn't be confined to only one part of the body and that it, in fact, should be moving throughout the body.

Always be present

The basic principle of all teachings is the need to be present in the moment. Present doesn't imply being present physically. It means being present mentally as well. You will have to be present in the moment. Don't let your mind or thoughts wander anywhere and don't fantasize about anything else apart from the activity that you are involved in at the moment. Be present in the moment with your partner, and be aware of what is happening.

It usually happens that people tend to zone off and are not present in the moment while having sex. They tend to close their eyes while having sex and their mind wanders to their fantasy realm instead of being present and being involved in the sexual activity that they are a partaking in. Sometimes, men tend to do this on purpose. Men tend to divert or distract themselves by thinking of different non-sexual things so that they can postpone their ejaculation. This practice isn't necessary when it comes to Tantra. If you want to experience every moment to the fullest, then you will need to be aware of what is happening around you. Your energy tends to follow the path of your attention and concentration. When your concentration wavers, the flow of energy in your body tends to waver as well. This will make you distracted and detached from the present scenario. Focus your energy on the act, on yourself, and your partner. Be in the moment, and don't lose focus of this.

Exploration of your senses

Tantra is an ancient art, and it's been around for centuries. It is crucial to take note of the fact that Tantra isn't just about improving the physical quality of having intercourse, but it is also about enhancing the emotional experience. All your sensory organs tend to take part in your sexual experience. Sex isn't an isolated process. Therefore, Tantra is all about improving your sensory experience as well. If one of your senses has been compromised then, the other senses tend to become sensitive.

Take inspiration from this, and you can probably incorporate this into any of the sexual encounters that you might have with your partner. It is not just about participating in the act; it is also important to explore all the senses of your partner and yourself. You both should be able to create an environment that will help you in igniting your sexual fires. You needn't try too hard to do this. The environment should be sexual and sensual. It should let you relax. You can try and blindfold your partner. This will help in stimulating their other sensory organs. You can tantalize their olfactory senses by incorporating various aromatic essential oils and scents into your routine. You can stimulate their sense of sound by playing some slow and soothing music, something that will build up some anticipation. Coming to the sense of taste, you can feed each other some luscious berries or even lick off some cream off their fingers. Various things can be done for stimulating one's senses. Tease their body and tease their senses as well. Let your imagination run wild, and there are no restrictions. You can caress their body with feathers, silk, or any other material. Once you have managed to tease all their senses, remove the blindfold and let your partner see what you have been up to. That smoldering look of unmistakable desire in their eyes would be amazing.

Aim for a full body orgasm

Who wouldn't want to have an orgasm? A full body orgasm does sound tempting, doesn't it? So, without wasting any time, let us get started with this fascinating concept.

One manner in which you can condition your body to have a full body orgasm is by practicing the build up to an impending orgasm and then letting it subside without giving in to the pleasure. You will have to drive your partner to the brink of an orgasm and then let it fade away, without letting them climax. Once you let it subside, you will have to start building it up again and let it fade away again. Use all your willpower and keep playing at it for as long as you possibly can.

You can take your partner to the brink of an orgasm orally or through any other method, but you should not give them the relief that they are craving for, at least not for a while. Keep building upon this pleasure. After keeping at it for a while, you can finally let go. Once your lover does get to experience the much-awaited orgasm finally, it will be truly spectacular.

The journey counts

Orgasms are wonderful, but Tantric sex isn't about simply achieving an orgasm. It is about delaying your orgasm for a while longer to receive better results. An orgasm can be thought of as a wonderful by-product of engaging in Tantric sex. Tantric sex is more spiritual and sacred than regular sex. It is the union of the opposing sexual energies present in the partners. The pressure of having to achieve an orgasm tends to take away the pleasure of participating in a sexual act. This stress is quite harmful, and it has a negative impact on the person's performance. The journey in Tantric sex is almost as important as a result. Orgasm isn't the main aim. It is about enjoying your body and your partner as well. It is about worshiping each other's bodies and cherishing your time together. Sex means so much more than a mere physical act that a couple would engage in. Try shifting your focus to different things that you enjoy and also the things that your partner finds pleasurable. There will certainly be certain things that you both seem to enjoy. Find those common things. It may be kissing, foreplay, holding each other or any oral activity and incorporate these into your lovemaking process.

Tricks for pleasure

The thigh high
Select your favorite essential oil and pour a few drops of this scented oil onto your hands. Make sure that your plasma are well oiled and then place these on your partner's thighs, a little above their knee. Start by gently kneading and move upwards. Take your time and let the anticipation build. This buildup of sexual tension will just add to the experience and

make it more pleasurable. Don't touch your partner's genitals; instead, focus on the areas around the genitals.

Take the nail road

Make use of your nails and gently trace patterns of figure eight on your lover's thigh or run your nails lightly along the length of their back or their calf. Tease all those areas that are sensitive to touch and vary the pressure to elicit different reactions from your partner.

Try the aural sex rub

Take some time and try and massage your partner's ear. Make sure that you are being gentle and make use of light touches. Use your fingers and start working from the outer fold of the ear towards the inner ear. Run your little finger along the outer edge of the finger. You can whisper sweet nothings and endearments into your partner's ear while doing this. You can gently lick and poke around with your tongue if you are feeling slightly adventurous.

Now, turn up the heat

After all the teasing and the tantalizing foreplay, it is time to turn up the heat. You and your partner can indulge in some oral sex or explore one of the many tantric sex positions that you have read about in the previous chapter. It is up to you, the manner in which you want to turn up the heat in the bedroom. Take your time as you did with all the foreplay. It isn't a quickie; it is about savoring the moment and honoring each other's bodies.

These principles will help you in improving your sexual experiences. Tantric sex is about engaging your senses and your consciousness in the moment and deriving the maximum pleasure you possibly can.

Chapter 12: Supplementary Activities to Improve Tantric Sex

The main purpose of Tantra is to help you achieve brilliant orgasms that you have been denied because of your regular sexual practices. However, this doesn't mean that Tantra should be treated lightly. Think of Tantra as a sensual workout. Tantric sex is considered to be more enjoyable than having to spend hours together at the gym, but the amount of physical exertion that your body experiences can be compared to that you might experience while performing any heavy exercises.

Moreover, there are different levels of Tantric sex. Simply jumping into Tantra without any experience or preliminary practice may make your sex life better, but it is so much better when you engage in some form of pre-sex warm up exercise that will help in setting the mood and building up some anticipation as to what is yet to come. There are several ways in which you can warm up, but possibly the best way possible would be to give your partner a massage and have your partner give you one as well. This will loosen up your muscles, which is important because stiff muscles can get in the way of a full body orgasm.

The massage that you are giving to prepare your lover for tantric sex has some specific rules that are attached to it, along with a technique that is designed to heighten the sexual sensitivity and make the body more receptive to further sexual stimulation. Also, this massage can be coupled with a technique that can be used on a woman to make her achieve an orgasm. This will contribute greatly to the quality of tantric sex because receiving one orgasm makes a person patient for the next one, and this provides you with the necessary opportunity o tease your partner and draw out the sex.

The Use of Oil

The first thing that you need before you can give your lover a pre-sex massage is oil. Oil is a great tool that can be made use of if you want your massage to be more effective. It helps in loosening the skin up and providing lubrication for your hands. If your hands can slide and glide smoothly across your lover's body more effectively, then it will also help in making the massage more sensual and helps in leading up to the actual sex!

The best oil that you can make use of in a pre-sex massage is grape seed oil. This is because grape seed oil has the least number of people that are allergic to it, and can be great for your skin. Thereby, by giving your lover a grape seed oil massage you are going to be helping him, or her get softer skin as well, and isn't this an excellent added bonus? You can always add a few drops of your favorite scented or essential oil to make the experience even better. Different essential oils can be made use of depending upon the particular reason for which it is being used. For instance, lavender can be made use of for relaxing and soothing muscles; rose can be made use of for giving a more sensual feel to the massage.

If grape seed oil is not available, go for any other oil that has been manufactured for the purpose of massages.

The Technique

The first thing that you will have to do is obviously start spreading the oil across your lover's body. Make sure that the oil is distributed evenly all over the body, and keep in mind that too little oil will not provide adequate lubrication and result in chaffing. However, making use of too much would just end up getting messy, and this can be annoying. Try to find the happy medium! While you are spreading the oil across your partner's body, you will find that the skin absorbs the oil very quickly. Hence, you will have to keep frequently spreading more oil across his or her body, if the lubrication stops being sufficient.

Once the oil has been spread across your partner's body, the massage can properly begin. Initially, it would be a good idea to start with basic compression of all of the major muscles. The muscle you should go for when applying wide and nonspecific compression are the thigh muscles because this area is usually under the most strain throughout the day.

Once the muscles have been loosened up in your partner's legs, you can move his or her back, the second-most tense area of the average body. Just apply pressure with your flattened palm, and remember to communicate with your partner as much as you can about what feels good and what is painful.

Try lightly slapping areas that you feel are already loose to stimulate blood circulation in these areas. Remember not to slap so hard that it hurts unless your partner wants you to of course!

Once you have completed this massage and loosened up the major muscle groups, it is time to begin focused compression with the tips of your fingers and your fists. There are specific areas that you should be targeting during focused compression, and these areas are specified in the next section.

Areas to Target

Breasts: The breasts are one particular area of the human anatomy that tend to attract a lot of attention, and it so happens, that they are also an excellent source of sexual stimulation for many people. They also tend to have very concentrated points of tension that, when released, end up making the person feel incredibly relaxed and peaceful.

Therefore, breasts are obviously going to be one of the most important areas of the body that you should target. Points of tension here are probably going to be on the lower half of the breasts. It is important that you feel around, trying to find the area where the tension exists.

This little ball of tension can be found right below the nipple, and your partner might probably cry out when you hit this particular spot. However, do not misinterpret this pain and stop the massage. This pain is very enjoyable, with many people comparing it to the feeling once gets while scratching an itch.

An important thing to note while performing such a massage is the origin of these little balls of tension that are present in the body. They are not simply muscular tension. Their origin is more metaphysical than physical in nature.

You are already familiar with the various chakras present in the body. However, you probably aren't aware that these chakras are the major stops in a vast network of energy that is flowing within your body, vortices through which energy constantly flows. However, there are certain situations where the flow of energy can get disrupted.

This usually happens due to a poor diet or an injury in a past life that might have a residual effect on your body in this life. As a result, when you apply deep pressure to these points the energy starts to get released, thus removing the obstruction that was previously blocking the flow of energy in your body.

Releasing energy is painful but at the same time quite enjoyable because the flow of energy provides vitality and increased sexual sensitivity to your body. This means that when you massage these points, your partner is going to feel an intense itching sensation that will devolve into a tickling sensation as the blockage is removed from the energy pathways in the body.

The best way in which you can apply pressure to this particular point is by pressing down using the tips of your fingers. Start by applying pressure and moving your hands in a circular motion. This will release the energy blockage in a very mild and efficient way. The circular motion loosens up stuck energy and then allows your hand to move away to a different part of the blockage, allowing the loosened up energy to flow into the energy pathway without being obstructed by the compression of your fingers.

You can also apply intense pressure to this point. This is very useful because it will release energy from the blockage in an extremely intense manner, and this will end up opening your partner up for intense sexual stimulation.

Butt: This is another area of the body that most people are very aroused by. As it turns out, the butt is just as prone to blockages in energy as breasts are, probably because of the intense amount strain they go through when the people they are attached to spend the vast majority of their day sitting in an office. With the amount of sitting that we do, it is no wonder that the pathways of energy in our derrieres end up getting backed up.

The important thing here is to feel your way around the area. Blockages can occur in several different parts of the butt, so you will have to poke around a little to find out where exactly the blockage has occurred. An odd little coincidence is that the energy blockage is probably going to occur in the same place on both cheeks, so if you find the spot on one cheek simply start pressing the same spot on the other cheek as well.

Apply the same circular motion with the tips of your fingers that you used on your partner's breast. These energy blockages might require some more pressure, however, so if your partner is unable to feel anything when you are massaging him or her, just trying using your thumb instead.

You might face difficulty finding the pressure point in this part of the body, especially if your partner has been gifted with a curvy backside. This is because the energy pathways are buried underneath a lot of flesh. Breasts rarely ever pose such a problem, even if the breasts in question are quite large.

This is because the pressure points located in breasts are not as deep as the ones in the backside. Hence, if you are facing difficult locating your partner's pressure point, use your thumb, and it will do the trick. If your thumb is still not sufficient, try using something rigid like a pen to apply pressure, just make sure you use the rear end of the pen and not the pointy end!

Using such a tool will help you to provide incredibly focused pressure onto the energy blockage, facilitating a very quick dissipation of energy and in the process probably turning your partner on a great deal.

Inner thighs: Finding the blockage in energy in this area of your body might turn out to be a lot more difficult than finding it on other parts of the body. This is why a perfunctory massage of the thighs is necessary before you begin to probe for pressure points.

The muscle massage is helpful because it will remove a lot of distractions from that general area. A lot of the time, you might be probing for the pressure point and would supposedly find it quickly, only to discover that it was just basic muscle pain and not the pain that stems from a blocked energy pathway.

However, if you have relaxed the muscles in your partner's thighs, the process should be a lot easier. One good tip that you should follow is to look for the pressure point in the upper inner thigh, which means the area of your thigh that is directly below your partner's crotch.

Try to squeeze this area generally to find a general location of the pressure point, and then narrow it down by using the tips of your fingers. When you find the pressure point, start applying the same circular pressure that you used to both the previous body parts.

Be mindful while applying pressure to the inner thighs. The pressure point here is a lot more delicate than the pressure points in the butt or even the breasts. Gentle pressure will get the job done, and apply too much pressure will just end up causing unnecessary pain that will probably force your partner out of the mood.

If the circular motion technique proves to be too intense for your partner, try moving your fingers forward as you gently massage the point instead. This will help by applying much gentler pressure than the circular motion, and the fact that it is much more sensual certainly doesn't hurt either!

Lower back: This area of the body is very different from the three areas discussed previously, and so will tackle in a manner that is completely different to the way that the previous body parts were tackled

What makes the lower back so unique is that it doesn't have a single point of energy blockage that you will have to focus on. Rather, you are partner will have one of two possible energy blockage situations, each of which has its specific technique that you can use to tackle it.

The first situation would be that there are several dozen separate points of energy blockage that are peppering across your entire lower back, being focused specifically on the section of your lower back directly before your butt along with the area of your lower back that is directly along your spine.

The second situation would be that the energy blockage would be spread out across the entirety of your lower back, with the energy nexuses interconnecting to form a network of blockages similar to the actual network of energy pathways that your body possesses.

The second situation is most often seen in women with large breasts and people who do a lot of manual labor. This is because such people tend to put a lot of strain on their lower back, forcing the energy pathways to get blocked because these strenuous activities would interrupt their circulation.

Overall, the lower back is always going to be a very serious place of energy blockage unless your partner gets regular massages, and the benefit of this is that even the slightest massage in this area will greatly stimulate your partner and will result in almost instant arousal if done right.

To find out which of the two-energy blockage situations your partner is suffering from you are going to have to probe quite a lot. Use your fingers to see where the energy blockages are. If there are spaces between the points where your partner feels pain, this means that the energy blockages that your partner is suffering from are separate from each other.

However, if every inch of your partners back aches when you massage it in that special itchy, tickly way, then your partner's energy blockage situation is of the second type.

The first situation is a lot more difficult to tackle than the second situation. Since the energy blockages are not connected, you are going to have to tackle each one individually rather than all at the same time. This is because attempting to massage several points at once could result in unpleasant pain for your partner.

However, solving this energy blockage situation is not that difficult once you get the hang of it. Simply press each pressure point and release the blockage by moving your hands in the circular motion that you will be familiar to by now. You will soon discover that once you take care of one blockage, the ones around it will begin to get weaker automatically.

This means that focusing on several important spots will allow you to dissipate the energy blockages and have the energy pathways flowing freely in no time.

The second situation, however, requires a very different approach. The first thing you must know about this approach is that it involves absolutely no subtlety. The energy blockage is severe and is going to get in the way of your partner's orgasm, and since the blockage is widespread and interconnected, the best thing that you can do is try to tackle at much of it at the same time as you can.

Warm up your partner's lower back by using your thumbs to ease the energy blockages into getting a little weaker. After a minute or two of this, you should begin using your fists.

Knead your partner's lower back as if it was dough. This may seem funny, but if you knead your partner's lower back exactly the way you would knead dough, with the quick movements and not staying in the same place for too long, your partner will soon be so relaxed that they'd feel as though they are floating away.

The second situation, although technically more severe, is a lot easier to dissipate than the first situation. Just make sure that you do not end up hurting your partner by applying too much pressure. Remember, communication is essential if you want to make sure that the massage experience is as enjoyable as possible.

You will find that no other area will provide as much sexual stimulation as the lower back as it is being massaged. This is because the energy that is being released is making them a lot more sensitive to sexual stimuli. Giving your partner a full body orgasm will become a lot easier after you have massaged her back to the fullest extent possible.

Feet and hands: Each and every body part that has been discussed in this section is important. Massaging these body parts is an essential part of preparing your body for the intensity of tantric sex. However, even though the lower back is home to the most severe energy blockage in your entire body, there are no parts of your body that is more important to massage than your hands and your feet.

This is because your hands and feet contain major energy pathways because so much energy is lost and gained through your extremities. Also, since you use your hands and feet so much, a lot of these energy pathways end up getting blocked.

This is particularly important to note because the pathway for pretty much every single organ in your body is present in your hands and feet. This means that easing the blockages out of the energy pathways in your hands and feet will help your body to become more sensitive to stimuli, making the climax of your lovemaking that much more intense.

Since the pathways in your partner's hand are so diverse and close to each other, you do not have to focus on each point individually. You can instead give your hands general massages as long as you make sure that you target every part of your hand during the massage.

However, as far as your partner's feet are concerned, a general massage won't do. The foot has separated clusters of energy pathway nexuses instead of the pointillist spread of nexuses that your hand has, which means that a general massage might help you loosen the muscles of your foot up but probably won't do much to free the energy blockages.

Hence, for your feet you are going to have to apply deep pressure using your thumb. The first area you should try is the upper center of your foot, as this area commonly has a cluster of energy blockages in it since so much strain is placed on it throughout the day.

After you have applied pressure and loosened up this energy blockage, you can begin exploring for more blockages. Other common areas include the heel and the big toe, with the little toes also having nexuses for minor energy pathways.

You can also use this technique on your partner's hands as well. Certain areas of your hand contain blockages for nexuses serving specific parts of the body. The body part that you care about right now is your partner's vagina, so naturally, you are going to want to massage a part of your partner's hand that would help to remove energy blockages leading to this all important part of your partner's anatomy.

The part of your hand that connects via energy pathways to your partner's vagina is the heel of her hand, which is the fleshy part of her hand underneath her thumb. Pressing down here will give your partner that itchy pain that comes with the pressing of pressure points, but that's not all it does.

Blocked energy pathways are a big contributor to your inability to bring your partner to orgasm. If no energy is reaching the area that so desperately needs the energy to climax, your partner will not have an orgasm no matter how many fancy tricks you try.

Hence, releasing the energy blockage from this part of your partner's hand will help make her vagina a lot more sensitive. The important part is that it will become sensitive all the way through, which is going to make her g spot, that rarely discovered fount of infinite ecstasy for women, a lot easier to find.

This easy discovery of your partner's g spot is going to prove immensely useful in the next part of the chapter, where a unique technique is going to be discussed that is going to give you the ability to provide your partner with mind blowing orgasms that will course through her entire body and potentially last for hours!

The Two Finger Jerk Technique

This is perhaps one of the most useful techniques that you can ever learn, and it is quite effective. There is no greater pleasure than in having the knowledge that you have managed to provide your partner with an intense orgasm. By making use of this technique, you will be able to help your partner achieve an orgasm that she will truly enjoy.

It is very important that you perform the massage properly for several days at least before trying this technique. It involves intense sexual energy, and attempting to do it while your partner's energy pathways are blocked can result in the energy congestion getting a lot worse than it was.

This is because this technique results in a veritable eruption of sexual energy from your partner's vagina at the time of the orgasm. Remember, these are full body orgasms that you are about to give your partner, so the sexual energy that she is about to emit is going to be intense.

Additionally, you are probably going to end up giving her far more than one orgasm. This technique will allow you to give her orgasm after orgasm, which means that the energy is not just going to be intense, there is going to be a lot of it coursing through her, so her energy pathways need to be clear.

Once you have given her the massage every day for at least a week, you will be ready to apply the technique. Give her the same massage to get her into the mood and get her as relaxed as possible. Remember, the more relaxed she is, the fewer blockages there are going to be during the act itself. Getting her nice and loose would mean that the orgasm would rip through her in no time.

Once the massage is finished, have her lie on her back, relax all of her muscles, and then spread her legs. Once her legs are spread, stimulate her vagina by rubbing it gently. You will notice that she is a lot more receptive to your touch right now. This is because her sexual energy is flowing a lot more freely than it was before, and as a result, her vagina is going to feel everything a lot more strongly.

Once you have stimulated her clitoris using your fingers, you must insert two fingers into her vagina. It is highly recommended that you face your palm upwards and insert your middle and ring fingers into it with your index and little fingers facing downwards and your thumb facing outwards.

Once you are in, you will have to jerk your hand upwards. Your fingers are going to be directly underneath your partner's G spot, a bundle of nerves that, when stimulated, can give your partner extremely intense orgasms. Jerking your hand upwards will press your inserted fingers against your partner's g spot, and you will immediately notice that there are waves of intense pleasure flowing across her body.

You can ease her into the process by stroking her G spot with your inserted fingers before you begin to jerk your hands upwards. Whatever you do, make sure that when you do jerk your hand upwards, you do it with moderate force.

You may feel as though your partner might get injured if you are too rough with her, but try not to worry about her vagina too much. After all, the vagina is where babies come from, which means that it is designed to be able to handle a bit of rough handling.

Not being forceful, enough would result in you not being able to stimulate her G spot. However, if you apply enough force, you are going to be able to make her orgasm within three minutes, and before your eyes, you are going to see the efficacy of this technique as your partner practically loses control of her limbs.

Once you give her the first orgasm, giving her, another orgasm is going to be very easy. All you will have to do is apply the same technique but for a much shorter period. Try to see how many times you make her orgasm before she can't take anymore, with this technique it'll be easy!

Conclusion

I would like to thank you once again for downloading this book.

I hope by now you will have understood the importance and need for a couple to engage in and be fully involved in their sexual experiences. In today's world, everything is being done in a hurry, in a rush. Whether it is our relationships, conversations, food or sex - regardless of what it is - everything is being done in a rush. Quickies and casual sex have become the norm of the day, and no one has got the time to engage in a sexual experience that transcends the physical boundaries.

Tantra includes a variety of topics and Tantric sex is perhaps the most popular one. Tantric sex is all about taking things slowly, savoring each moment and enjoying the experience. It's not about attaining an orgasm, but it is about enjoying each other. Different techniques of meditation, exercises and sexual positions will help in deepening the bond between the partners and it will help in improving the intimacy quotient in the relationship.

I hope this book serves as a basic guide to Tantric sex. If you follow the various practices mentioned in this book, then you will see a positive change in your sex life. Lovemaking is so much more than just the physical act of sex; it involves forming a bond with your partner. Initially, you will need to consciously make sure that you are following the steps mentioned in this book but, over a period of time, all this will come naturally to you. If you want to see some positive results, then you will need to put in considerable time and effort into this process. It will take a while to get the hang of these techniques, so don't get disheartened, and keep trying. Thank you and all the best

Printed in Germany
by Amazon Distribution
GmbH, Leipzig